White Sand

&

Wild Strawberries

Kathy J. Kunkel Magnus

For My Family

Dick

Erica, Eric, Cory, Jill

Josh, Zach, Ben, Meron

Jackson, Tucker and Ryder

You light up my life.

XOXO

Thanks

Great thanks to the wonderful women in my Writer's Group – Judy Pett, Karen Boyum, Vicki Norstog, and Bev Luttio who encouraged, proofed, critiqued and never stopped pushing me to be a better writer; to Liz Peterson who knew where to put the commas; to my readers and advice givers – especially Erica Koser, Jill Magnus, Sherrie Kunkel, Joan Graham, Else Thompson and Myrna Sheie; and to my husband Dick who encourages, appreciates, and is always my best sounding board.

CONTENTS

NATURE

..

Photo credits:
Erica Koser, Page 8
Pixabay, Pages 29, 45, 82
Richard Magnus, Pages 101, 129
Jill Magnus, Page 132

Introduction

In the past couple of years I've taken the opportunity to dig deeply into memories and musings -- growing up on a lake in Central Minnesota, spending time with my grandmothers, becoming a mother and a grandmother myself, and the joys and challenges of adult life. I've delighted in memories of fishing with my dad, walking along an ocean beach in the fog, and even encountering Big Horn sheep up close and personal on an early morning hike. I recalled life experiences such as how much I loved our small town library, how I delight in watching a summer storm move in, and how difficult the reality is of losing beloved elders.

I've remembered places, people and emotions. As I wrote, I rediscovered the joy and beauty of the every-days. Whether recalling an interesting walk with a grandchild, standing on a dock in a Swedish harbor, a well-spent afternoon with a friend, or my brother's habit of eating the top off my Dairy Queen, these are my stories.

I hope some of these stories ring true for you and open some of your own treasured memories.

Growing Up
On the
Lake

I Am From

White sand and gently lapping lakeshore
Laundry, crisp and flapping in early morning sun
Fat red geraniums and elegant purple gladiolas
Laughter, and coffee with cream
Familiar hymns at the piano
Sweet, ripe tomatoes and freshly-picked raspberries
Old wooden fishing boats on Saturday afternoons
Sandburs and wild Black-eyed Susans
Black and white photos
Stories, books, journals, daydreams
Beauty and safety, loss and tears
I am from love.

Summer's First Gift

A narrow hard-packed dirt path
Leads from my house to the lake.
Lined with tall majestic oaks,
Acorn shells crunch under my feet as I walk.

Scrub oak and sumac bushes
Snag at my red cotton shirt.
Dappled sunlight plays on the leafy forest floor.
The smell is heavy, sweet, damp and green.

My dirt path gives way to soft, white sugar sand
And slopes steeply down to the lakeshore.
Sandburs attach themselves to my shoelaces.

As I reach down to pull the burrs off,
My hand encounters a tiny, wild strawberry plant.
Four perfect, petite strawberries waiting just for me.

Sinking into the warm welcoming sand I gently pick all four.
Their sweet smell is heady and intoxicating.
I pop them one by one into my mouth.

As the tiny strawberries melt in my mouth
I experience a moment of sheer bliss.

Ah, summer's first gift.

Lake Girl

Coming down the path I smell the lake before I see it.
My feet pick up speed over the last sand dune
And there it stretches before me,
My lake.

My mother and younger brother behind me,
We traipse to the beach and dump
Towels, thermos, nose plugs, swim masks,
Pails, shovels and snacks on the sand.

My lake is shallow and crystal clear
With a rippling sandy bottom.
I can walk out 50 yards
And still not be over my seven-year-old head.

I pull on my green rubber swim mask and tighten the strap.
Skipping into the cool water
My splash breaks the mirror-smooth surface.
I run until the water tickles my knees.

Lying face down in the water
I spy a school of darting minnows.
A clam moves ever so slowly on his way.
I decide not to bother him today.

I flip to my back and stretch out.
Half floating, half lying on the sandy lake bottom
I look up now instead of down
And watch fleecy clouds play in the warm sun.

In a minute I'll go in and build a sand castle.
Or maybe I'll walk out all the way to my waist.
Or maybe not. It's my lake.

A Creamsicle Please

Whatever happened to summer evening car rides?
Before air conditioning, remember?
The air in the house was sticky and oppressive,
Cooled only by the small whirring blue metal fan
In the window.

The annoying, droning buzz of a loopy fly
Kamakazying itself into the window.
Mom didn't want to cook
So we had delicious, messy BLTs,
And lemonade instead of milk.

Sometimes if we were lucky,
After supper our parents would suggest
A ride to cool us off before bed.

Going for a ride held promise.
Going for a ride meant all four car windows rolled down,
Summer evening air blowing into my face
And blowing my hair straight back.

It meant sharing the backseat with my brother
But since we were both hanging out the windows
There were no arguments
About who was taking up more space.

A ride could mean following a winding, country, dirt road
To a lake where we would wade in the shallow water
And accidentally get very wet.

A ride could mean stopping at the Ossipee Store for a treat.
Our country store sold bread, milk, fishing worms,
Cigarettes, candy, and ice cream.
The owner, Mr. Waffensmith, lived behind the store.

In winter, spring and fall, when I entered the store
My eyes focused on the three shelves behind the counter
Filled with candy bars, Lifesavers, bubble gum.

But on a muggy, hot summer night
The focus was the counter-high
Metal-topped, red, refrigerated chest.
When Dad slid its top door open,
Cold air rushed up into my face.
Bliss.

Choices were
Ice cream bars
Creamsicles
Push-ups
Popsicles.

An orange Creamsicle, please.

A perfect end to a sultry summer day.
Life was safe and uncomplicated.
Gas was 25 cents a gallon.

Whatever happened to summer evening car rides?

Dining Pleasures

A bright blue metal lunch box
Matching two-cup thermos inside
My name inked on adhesive tape near the handle
One hard-boiled egg
Mom's penciled note on the shell
One sweet smelling pear, a little bruised
One peanut butter and honey sandwich
Crusts removed
Cold chocolate milk
First Grade lunch.

My Perch

My yard is filled with giant oaks
Abundant providers of
Acorns
Homes for countless birds and squirrels
Soft green buds in early spring
Crunchy red leaves in autumn
Dry sticks for campfires
Green sticks for roasting marshmallows
Leafy dense shade in hot summer sun.

But their best gift?
The low, sturdy branch I climb
To my perch where I contentedly sit
To watch my world from the gray squirrel's perspective.

Oak Trees and Dirt Roads

Our lake house sits far back from the tar road,
Sheltered by giant oaks.
Coming down State Road 3
You will know to slow down
When you see five gray, metal mailboxes all in a row.

One for us
One for the resort down the gravel road
One for old Mr. and Mrs. DeNapoli
(He of the always-lit cigar)
One for the summer cabin
One for Mr. Shafer
(He of the shiny 1950 black Hudson)

We have our own dirt driveway.
More a lane than a proper drive,
Weeds grow down the middle of the two tracks.
When a car drives up you can hear acorns pop and crunch.

My favorite uncle came to visit.
He drives a convertible.
All afternoon we heard acorns dropping onto the hood
And the seats.

We all laughed.
I made him fudge.

First Memories

Sunshine streams in a kitchen window,
Wooden alphabet blocks form a long, winding road
Across the shiny red linoleum floor.

I take my small dime store turtle
From his glass terrarium bowl, and
Place him on the first block of my road.

Unsuccessfully, I encourage him to make his way.
He topples. He falls.
We try again
And again
And again.

Famine or Feast?

No library within thirty miles.
I've read and reread my shelved books.
I'm dying of boredom.
I need something to read.

Dragging my feet down our dirt driveway,
My task is to get the mail.
The take-out is meager.
Bills, advertisements,
McCall's magazine.
And then – a feast appears.

My Summer Weekly Reader!
Eight pages of stories, cartoons,
Games, riddles, hidden pictures, project ideas.

I dash to the house,
Dump mail on the dining room table
And settle into the big chair, my legs draped over the arm.

I begin to devour it
And then slow to a delightful, filling, hour-long banquet.
"Hungry yet, Honey?"
"No, Mom. I'm good. Maybe later."

Front Lawn Picnic

Red Keds
Red terrycloth shorts
A top made from two red bandanas stitched together
Too-short bangs
A flower barrette holding back my dark hair.

Mom spreads the blanket on the lawn.
Two bronze-colored metal glasses with ice cubes
And orange Kool-aide,
Butter and sugar sandwiches on crustless white bread,
A pear.

On my tummy,
My face off the blanket's edge
Nose down in the sweet smelling grass
I search for four-leaf clovers.

Trying to improve on perfection.

Lifesavers

Summer Saturday morning -
Sunshine kisses me warmly from nose to toes,
Our old wooden fishing boat stands ready.

The Bait Shop -
Dusky, smelling of stale cigarettes, fish, summer
A baseball game on the radio
Dad buys a small cardboard container of worms
And I buy one roll of Butter Rum Lifesavers.

The Crow Wing River -
The river my dad has fished since he was a child
Soaring eaglets, sunning turtles,
A small, sun-dappled cove with overhanging birch branches

Going fishing -
No fishing pole, just a four-inch-long wooden stick,
Ten feet of fishing line wrapped around it
A sinker, a bobber and a hook.
I thread a wiggly, slimy worm on the hook
And toss the line into the water.

Lazy sunshine on my back -
Waiting
Nibble, nibble. *Jerk*
Nibble, nibble. *Jerk*
Mosquito. *Slap*
My reflection shimmers on the still water
Got one!
Time for a Butter Rum Lifesaver

Thread another worm on the hook
Try again.
Nibble, nibble
Daydream
Jerk
Nibble, nibble.

Grin.

County Fair

Hot popcorn and the sticky sweet smell of pink cotton candy
Mingle with pungent odors from cattle barns.
Hucksters beckon me with promises,
Flashy lights illumine the Midway.
Five dollars in my pocket,
I'm ready for adventure.

We tour the 4-H building as a family.
Countless adult acquaintances stop to chat.
"Haven't seen you since last year's fair.
Your kids have sure grown."
I silently endure and await freedom.
Finally Mom says,
"Meet us at the Lutheran church building for pie in 45 minutes."

I'm off!
Caramel apple in hand
I stroll the Midway inhaling essence d'fair:
Dust, sawdust, sweat, roasting hot dogs, good fortune.
I fail at tossing a hoop over a milk bottle
Fifty cents gone
Fifty cents gone for a ride on the Tilt-a-Whirl.

Finding a friend
We ride the Ferris wheel
The bumper cars
Buy a grape ice
See that 8th grade boy I might like
Watch him shoot metal ducks on a wheel.

Check my watch.
Banana cream pie time.

Next year will I be old enough to come to the fair by myself?

Friday Night Special

One yellow and red box on the pink Formica countertop.
A large mixing bowl, a wooden spoon, and
A well-used cookie sheet.

Boxed ingredients include
Dough mix, tomato sauce
And a packet of smelly, grated cheese.

Add water and mix to create sticky dough
Spread the stickiness on the cookie sheet
Ladle on tomato sauce, top with grated cheese.
Bake.

Fill the good green glasses with ice cubes from their metal tray
Pour Pepsi to the top of each glass.
Turn on console television in living room.

Set up two metal TV trays
Take out four brown and gold Melmac plates
Put one plate on each TV tray, and
Two plates on the floor in front of the TV.

Timer Bell!
Remove the golden brown, crispy crusted meal from the oven.
Inhale the tomato-y, spicy, smoky, peppery smell of 'gourmet'
pizza

Cut into 20 squares with scissors from the junk drawer.
Carry hot cookie sheet into the living room and set it on the
floor.

With a spatula carefully serve
Two pieces to Mom
Two pieces to Dad
Two pieces to my brother
Two pieces for me.
For starters.

Just in time.
The theme song from Bonanza bursts from the TV, and
Pa, Adam, Hoss and Little Joe ride into our living room.

Friday night late dining at 7:00 p.m.
Extra-large Chef Boyardee pizza
Icy Pepsi in our glasses
An hour of western drama ahead of us.

Doesn't get any better than this.
Never has. Never will.

Creative Gardening

The last bits of produce are harvested from the huge garden
Red maple leaves flutter down and gather in the well-kept rows
Peas, beans, carrots, radishes, tomatoes, gone.

The first frost has changed the landscape.
Pumpkins and squash are now the produce d'jour,
Unharvested, decaying cucumbers still cling to their vines.

Plump, squishy cucumbers
No longer crisp but slimy
Worthless
Except…

I harvest thirty or more.
My ratty old sneakers
Stomp, smash, pulverize them.

I slide. I glide.
I pirouette.
I'm a daring eight-year-old skater
On an early autumn cucumber rink.

Slipped.
Yuck.

Family

My Dad Taught Me To

Go to church on Sunday
Grow tomatoes
Spit watermelon seeds
Respect my parents
Enjoy reading
Find a hobby
Paddle a canoe
Fish for sunnies
Climb a mountain
Cherish my sibling
Hunt for agates
Float on a lake
Change a tire
Marvel at a sunset
Yearn for travel and make it happen
Spend only what I have
Have a few good friends
Work hard
Save
Be a good neighbor
Grill a chicken
Pitch a tent
Plant a garden
Be thankful

Gone Missing

Too many of my beloved elders
Have spent difficult months
Held in dementia's prison.

Beloved elders
Who laughed with me
Played with me
Loved me.
Now gone missing.

Even though their smiles are here
Their voices are here
Their laughter is here
They are gone.

I visit.
Bring a treat to share,
Talk aloud in a one-sided conversation
Making no connection.
Sometimes we sing a song together.
Not always.

Time to leave.
I wrap her in a giant hug.
She says,
"I have no idea who you are, but I'm very sure I love you."
I know.
But the tears still roll down my cheeks and off my chin.
"I love you too. So very much.
See you soon."

Bruce

I was almost five when he came cooing and smiling,
Sliding into my space.
He was small, not much to worry about at all.
Except he got so much attention
Always hungry
Always wet
Always needing to be held.

But then, I got to hold him.
I sang him songs,
I cuddled him, and when he cried
I gave him back.

At night I was sometimes allowed to climb into his crib
And sing him songs until he went to sleep.
I was a good babysitter. A good big sister.

He grew.
He had friends. I had friends.
He had homework. I had homework.
We shared day-to-day life in family.
We shared family vacations and holidays
Going our own ways, but always there for each other.

I grew.
I left for college and realized how much I missed him.
We wrote letters. A few.
Coming home for a weekend
I would pick him up outside his junior high
We'd go to King Louie's for fries and Cokes and conversation.

We grew up, started families of our own
Living far from one another but
Held together by the threads of a lifetime.
Shared memories
Shared stories
Shared values
Shared hard decisions

And now
Best friends, but better.
Brother and sister.
Talking often, laughing much.
Cherishing time together.

But, still my little brother.
Still trying to bite the curlicue off my DQ.

Fried Potatoes

We ate them with sausage.
Always.
Thinly sliced
Fried until brown
They hissed in the hot oil as Mom sliced them
Into the black cast iron skillet.
Salt. Pepper. Sizzle.

The best ones turned crispy around the edges.
Never eaten with catsup as the neighbors did
But with light corn syrup.

They don't taste the same in my kitchen.
Is it the absence of the cast iron skillet?
Or the absence of Mom?

Fading Memories

I kept a bottle of her favorite lotion for years
But I can no longer remember her scent.
I have her collection of scarves, but rarely wear one.
I can't remember her voice.

Her costume jewelry is in a baggie
In the bottom of my lingerie drawer.
I wear three pieces of her good jewelry
But I can't remember her voice.

I do remember warm hugs and the songs she loved.
I know I was a well-loved daughter.
I pass a mirror and sometimes she looks back at me.
But after all these years,
I'd love to hear her voice.

First Dance

My first real dance
The Ninth Grade Spring Dance
Not formal, just a pretty spring dress
We shopped, Mom and me.
Even went to a neighboring town to find the perfect dress.

It was blue and white gingham with puffy sleeves
A dropped neckline with a lacy inset
Fitted at the waist, flared at the knee
An absolutely perfect dancing dress.

Mom had minor surgery and couldn't be home to help get me dressed
Dad took me up to the hospital so she could be part of the Big Event
She loved the dress
She loved the touch of make-up and
The sweet powder-blue shoes we had picked
I pirouetted around her hospital bed
We laughed.

I vaguely remember the decorated junior high gym
I vaguely remember the boy
I will never forget the week.
My mom died a short four days later from a massive infection.

I've lost most memory of the months that followed.
I know we moved ahead, my dad, my little brother and me.
I don't recall how.

Now decades later
I still mourn
She was 42
She never saw me grow up
She wasn't there to help plan my wedding
She never heard the news that she had become a grandma
Or see me strive to balance career and motherhood.

But she has been my role model
As a mother
A wife
A working mom
A woman of faith

I miss you, Mom.

Boulder River

We arrived at the cabin at sunset last night.
Autumn's golds and deep greens shimmered on the mountain,
Herds of deer and elk welcomed us.
My brother and sister-in-law's cabin
On Montana's Boulder River
Just a few miles down valley from Box Canyon
Where my father always hunted elk.

This morning we have come to Box Canyon's trailhead.
We drove up the rough and rutted gravel mountain road
Watching the river rush and splash down the mountain.
The meadow where Dad always pitched his tent
Bursts with butterflies, grasshoppers, wildflowers.

Two summers ago we scattered his ashes here.

Tall, slender, lodge-pole pines cover the mountainside
The smell is heady with the sweet fragrances of
Earth, water, wildflowers and pine.
The guys set out to hike up-canyon.

We sisters-in-law walk the short distance to the river's edge
To set up our day-camp:
Two lawn chairs
An old quilt
Water bottles
Fruit
Trail mix
Sandwiches
Cookies
Bug spray
Books and cameras.

The old quilt is spread over pine needles and twigs
Our chairs face the morning sun
We drink in the warmth.
What books are you reading?
How are the kids?
Grandkids?
Are you enjoying work?
Are you planning vacations?
Remember when…?

Cameras come out as a huge bird lands in the water
Snap. Snap. Snap.
We got it!

Our books lie at our feet unopened.
We sit statue-still
As a doe walks ever so near.
She stops by the river for a late morning drink.
Snap. Snap. Snap.
We got her!

Our table on the river bank
Has no plates, no goblets,
No table!
Our feast is for all the senses.
Most importantly it is a space for
Sharing time
Sharing stories
Sharing laughter
And a few tears.

A dining space to be remembered.
A family place to be remembered.

Just Yesterday

Home from the hospital swaddled in soft flannel blankets.
Holding this fragile little person closely
I sang, I cooed, I got teary.
This was my child!

She looked right into my eyes as if trying
To unlock mysteries of time and space.
I knew she could not yet even focus,
I didn't care.
This was my child!

I couldn't get enough of him.
Holding, rocking, touching, kissing that perfect head.
Exhausted.
Wouldn't have given it up for the world.
This was my child!

Celebration! She rolled over
Photos and movies. His first steps.
She ate only bananas and donuts.
He loved everything on his high chair tray.

Preschool – she learned songs and made new friends.
He ran dump trucks around the living room floor.
Kindergarten, First Grade
Discovering the world wasn't always kind.

Homework, field days, concerts, plays,
Sleep overs, birthday parties,
Visits from beloved grandparents,
Vacations.

Canoe trips on the Pine with Grandpa.
Best of times with cousins, aunts and uncles.
Grandma's treasure drawer and attic.
The best of being family

Popcorn by the fireplace.
Football in the fall.
Time to laugh and grow.
Home -- a safe place in a big world.
Junior high, high school
Opportunities to explore gifts and skills
Theater and music for her
Lacrosse and leadership for him.

College.
Each chose a place that fit,
But oh, so far from me.
Just yesterday they were swaddled in flannel.

Graduations, careers, relationships
A bride
A groom
Our family grew.

Now my babies have babies.
A whole new set of soft flannel blankets
A whole new set of miracles.

And it begins again.

The Everydays

Our first date, an icy January night,
A concert, a coffee, a conversation.
His worldview, values, dreams
So much like mine.

A year later we married,
Candlelight and roses in church
Surrounded by family and friends
We pledged our love.

Fast the time goes

Grad school
First careers
A new exciting city
Our first home
Birth of two children

Fast the time goes

Family times
Good friends
Saturday mornings
Good books
Good movies
Career moves
Quiet times on a mountain side
Popcorn by the fire
Hotdog roasts in spring
Watching waves by the shore
Turning leaves
Blowing snow

Holidays
Everydays

Fast the time goes

Kids grow
Kids become grown ups
Kids become parents.

I reflect and acknowledge
It's the common Everydays
I'm giving thanks for.
The Everydays I cherish.
The Everydays I miss most.

I wish I had known.

A Gift of Marriage

We married brothers
And became friends.
We married brothers
And became sisters.

Through the years we've
Delighted in our friendship
Loved each other's children
Agreed that our shared in-laws were the best
Traded recipes
Shared secrets
Marked milestone events
Shopped together
Shared favorite books and authors
Enjoyed a donut or two
Took vacations together
Wept together
Laughed together
Written letters
Sent emails
Understood each other

We married brothers
And became friends
We married brothers
And became sisters.

Nature

Spring

Promises

Snow, no longer the pristine white of winter
Now filthy slush
Slops up on my slacks as I walk
Cars send mucky spray in all directions
Bedraggled holiday wreaths cling to porch doors.

Winter is surely over, but where is Spring?

And then,
Poking its lovely purple face through the sloppy snow
A hyacinth.

It is enough for today
It is a promise of what is to come
Perhaps next week the tidal wave of spring
Will rush in with green and yellow, blossoms and fragrance.

I do believe in promises.

Spring Delay

The tulips are up about two inches
Sedum on the rock wall is greening up
The crab apple's pink blossoms are ready to burst.

A spring wreath graces my neighbor's front door
Evening is longer with Daylight Savings time
I fix chili for the last time until late fall.

Down jackets lie folded in boxes
Deck furniture emerges from winter wraps
Robins and goldfinches appear at the bird bath.

So why is a blizzard of quarter-sized snowflakes
Turning my beautiful spring green to white?
Stop!
This is totally unacceptable.

Maybe tomorrow the robins will be back?

Early March

Snowing again
Snowing still
Snowing more
Snowing hard
Snowing pretty
Snowing deep

Enough.

Sky Poems

Heavy spring rains and gusty winds
Stormed across the city last night.
Early morning skies are scoured azure blue.

Wispy clouds
Look like giant punctuation marks
Strewn across the sky.
Exclamation marks, dashes, semi-colons and question marks.

The beginnings of a sky poem?
Or just my whimsy?

Finding Spring

With the sun finally far enough north to warm the patio,
Donned in jeans and sweatshirts
We push winter into the past.

Time to pull winter coverings off the furniture,
Sweep away leaves, spider webs, and hidden acorns.
Patio chairs are carried to the lawn,
Scrubbed and dried.
Glass-topped cocktail tables are cleaned top to bottom
The patio floor is hosed corner to corner and back again,
Disturbing spider egg sacks and the
Skeletal remains of frightful insects.

The sun, just faintly warm this April morning,
Holds a promise for the weeks ahead.
Afternoons with lemonade and cookies,
Dinners with meat and vegetables grilled to perfection,
Long evenings reading books as the sun hangs forever
In the western sky.

Warm enough to have our first lunch of the season
On the patio today?
Moving chairs into the square of available sun
We vote Yes!

And Spring begins.

Quiet Morning

Thick morning fog bumps into my trees, my house.
Familiar with all my nooks and crannies
It sits plumply on my street.
A fat gray cozy comforter
With not one shred of energy.

I'll sit with my coffee and my book
Content
Until this old friend saunters off up and over the hill.

The Gardener's Calendar

February
The vision begins.
I envision bursts of red, orange, purple and yellow.
I sketch. I make lists. I wait.
Snow. More snow.
Wind chill. Bone chill.
Popcorn and fireplace crackle.
I wait.

May
List in hand, I enter the garden shop.
Three of these, three of these.
A flat of these.
My cart so full it wobbles down one more aisle.
Oh, definitely one of these!
And that one too.

In my yard with
Shovel, spade, garden gloves and dirt
I check my sketches.
What was I thinking?
No, not there!
But here. Here is where you belong.

I wait again as the earth continues to warm
And embraces my pregnant flower beds.

July
Bursts of red, orange, purple and yellow.
A feast for the eyes each morning.
I might need something taller there next year.
Perhaps I should start a list?

Summer

Sunrise

Early morning on the dock
Hot coffee steams in my white pottery mug.
The lake is still
A seagull flies along the distant shore
Not a boat to be seen.

Ten feet from my chair a fish jumps and
Launches six perfect ripples.
Now gone.
Quiet.

I wait in stillness for the loon's call.
It doesn't disappoint.
Natures comforting 'Up North' musical has begun.
An eagle joins the score.
I have a front row seat for this production.

Cherished moments of solitude
As the day gently breaks.
Time for emptying
Before the day fills me up.

Summer Storm

Heavy dark clouds
Laden with moisture
Thunder rolling, rumbling
Air so hot and humid it sticks to my skin
I can smell the coming rain.

The covered patio,
Open on two sides, beckons.
I settle into the comfy patio chair,
A frosty glass of lemonade in my hand.
I wait.

Neighborhood children are called inside
Birds stop singing
Frogs stop croaking
Chipmunks scamper across the rocks one last time.

The stillness is awesome.
I hear it begin.
Splats of heavy rain
Fall straight to the ground.
Faster and faster they come.
Sheets of rain
Beat down the grass,
Weigh down the shrub branches,
Flowers in my garden bow their heads.

I observe from my chair just inches from the raindrops.
I am part, and yet apart.
The rumble deepens
The smell is delicious, fresh, clean.
I breathe deeply.

I give thanks for
Summer storms
Cool rain quenching thirsty lawns and gardens
Cool rain quenching me.
.

Summer Friend

Lush greens of mid-summer surround me
The lake shimmers in the hot afternoon sun,
Frogs croak lazily,
Two cardinals chat with each other,
A speedy chipmunk races in front of me
On his way home to stash acorns
My walking path is rich in summer treasures.

An iridescent green dragonfly lights on my forearm.
I don't brush her off
But offer a free ride for the next mile.
I hum a favorite tune and she sits to listen.
My mind moves to list-making and she flits away.

She re-joins me on my shoulder,
So light I can't feel her.
So glorious in her green
She hovers around my head, and
Flies to the brim of my visor.
Perhaps a better vantage point?
We move along the path companionably.

Some days she would be a pest.
Today she is an elegant friend
Sharing a lovely summer afternoon.

Hush

Mother Nature is speaking.
Quiet, Self.
Hush, road sounds.
What is she telling today?

Frogs in the nearby marsh
Strike up an orchestral melody.
A loon calls in the distance
And another answers
Two squirrels chatter incessantly high in the tree.

Hush.
Close my eyes.
I hear a bee,
The muted croak of a toad on my deck,
A robin's splash in the bird bath.

Could I be quiet enough
To hear the earthworm as she
Pokes her head up in my flower bed?
Or the twitch of the bunny's nose?

Be still.
Listen.
Wait.
Eyes closed.
Mother Nature is speaking in magnificent tones.

Afternoon in a Hosta Garden

Dappled sun shines through huge, old oak trees
This sultry summer afternoon.
We sit on a worn, wooden bench in the arboretum
In a quiet, secluded oasis of hosta plants.
The smell of the damp, rich earth is heady.
Fat, slow-moving bumble bees fly sluggishly around us
Flying as if they are drunk on summer.

My friend and I meet here
Away from emails and busy lives
Sharing smoked almonds, dark chocolates
And a thermos of icy lemonade.

Old friends.
No agenda
No big announcements
Girl talk
Recipes
Movies
Children
Vacations
Faith
Books
Work
Travel

The laughter is genuine
The silent spaces comfortable
Old friends
Sharing small moments
Carved out of life
Moments captured in a hosta garden
With chocolate, honey bees, and stories.

Beach Fog

It's early.
The tide is out and the expanse of sandy beach beckons.
Fog rolled in early this morning,
The sea is shrouded in a gentle hug of gray.

I walk down the 100 stair steps
From my beach nest on the bluff.
The dampness of early morning fog,
Mist and sea-spray softly sprinkle my face.
I breathe deeply and listen to the call of the sea.

I know this beach.
I know its caves, curves and bluffs.
Today it is uncharted territory.
I can't see more than 30 feet in front of me,
There is no one here but me.

Wet sand
Pounding surf
Yet serene peacefulness
On this empty beach.

My mind empties and my soul opens.
Breathe.
Listen.
Hold this contentment.

Soon the sun will burn off the fog.
Pails, shovels, picnics and wave-jumping will fill this space.

But right now it is all mine.
Just mine
I think I'll sit a bit in the damp sand and
And let the fog envelop me in a hug.

Recipe for an Afternoon

Combine:
Two small boys
One large empty beach
Ample sand, shells, rocks, crabs,
Cliffs, seagull feathers and crashing waves.

Explore crevices, nooks, crannies
Collect pockets full of shells, sea debris, sticks.
Whisk in a little danger with crashing waves.

Mix well with sand castles and beach tag.
Bake in the warm sun until well-tired and
Covered with sand.

Enjoy the memories forever.

Interruption

Gentle, giant rumblings
Clouds far in the distance
I sit under the tree lost in my book
Icy lemonade at my side.

Blue sky fades to gray
Too content to move,
I am aware of a stillness that swallows up my neighborhood.
Three more pages.

Sizzle!
Jagged light cracks open the sky.
Crash!
The earth shakes its displeasure.

Huge raindrops pelt my body as I run.
Inside, I stand transfixed at the window,
Senses alert,
Hairs on my arms stand up.

Summer storm.

Oh I Do Love Summer

Bird song symphonies at 5:00 a.m.
Morning coffee on the deck
Plump blueberries
Freshly mown grass
Crisp watermelon cubes
Pink peonies
Icy root beer floats
Robins' eggs
Picnic baskets
Hot dogs at the baseball game
Grape popsicles
Juicy ripe tomatoes
Hammocks
Dairy Queen
Boat rides
Steaks on the grill
Corn on the cob
Sunscreen
S'mores
Docks
Bare toes
Fat, lazy bumblebees
Butterflies
Outdoor concerts
Twilight strolls
Long days
Loon calls
Fireflies

Ah, Summer!

Fall

Autumn Announcements

A cloudless blue sky
The buzz of a fat bumble bee paying a visit to my last tomato
Bright yellow mums in an old ceramic pot on the front step
Maples decked out in brilliant red
An autumn wreath on the front door
Glossy Honeycrisp apples in a bowl
Plump, juicy, purple grapes hang heavily in the arbor
Dry yellow leaves float to the ground
A vase of bittersweet sits on the table
Red and gold oak leaves crunch underfoot
A sumac bush bursts with its deep red leaves
Noisy, honking geese fly over
Frenzied chipmunks collect and bury acorns.

A simply delicious day!

September Thirty

Brilliant blue sky,
Rustling brown leaves crunch under my feet.
Warm. No need for a sweater.
Fragrance of spent blooms in a faded red pottery container.
A perfect autumn day.

Why do I feel I'm about to slide off a cliff
And crash into a whole new season?
A time when a sweater won't be enough
When a space heater replaces the fan
When stew sounds better than shrimp salad
When I wish for a mug of hot chocolate, not an icy lemonade?

I've been there before.
Days with crisp floating snowflakes
Blustery winds driving me to the fireplace with a good book.
Shoveling instead of weeding,
Bouquets from the florist, not my garden.

I take a deep breath.
October is hours away!
Accept what is,
And what will be.

The Five

A weekend conference
High in the Rocky Mountains.
I wake early to walk in the fresh fall morning
Foggy air hangs heavily
Wrapping me in solitude.

I walk the trail in the early quiet.
No voices, no cars, no music.
Just me and a rugged old mountain trail.

A bend in the trail
And there they are.
Five Big Horn sheep not more than fifty feet away.
The fog floats around their majestic curved horns.
I stand in awe, a bit fearful.
Their keen senses take in my unfamiliar scent.
They look at me, and
Unimpressed, they walk away.

A tear traces down my cheek
And my heart hammers in praise of creation.
No camera needed
I will never forget.

Summer Mourning

I've come to the beach to mourn.
One last day to sit in my faded beach chair
Toes in the sand
Watching waves rhythmically wash ashore
The sun, warm on my face.

I've come prepared.
Blue jeans, and a soft, warm sweatshirt,
Lunch – some cubes of cheese, a pear and a few crackers.
A book.

Hopeful seagulls spot my lunch, then ignore me.
No gourmet picnic for them today.
They are used to better fare from me,
They stare with disdain and squawk among themselves.

I open my book, but my eyes are drawn to sand and water.
A few brave sailboats skim the surface in search of summer.
The lifeguard station stands, a lonely sentinel,
One seagull perches on the top-most rung.

Gone is the smell of suntan lotion.
No children chase shore birds.
Sand no longer burns the bottoms of my feet.
Sandcastle builders have retired.

I'm not alone on this crisp October morning.
A young woman at the shoreline practices Tai Chi,
An elderly woman sits on a bench staring out at the water,
A long, knit scarf wound round her neck.
A young couple snuggles under a blanket,
A bikini-clad teen sunbathes in defiance of the chill.

Just us, bidding farewell.
Soaking up the last crumb of beach time.
Not yet ready for the brisk winds and
Gun-metal gray skies of November.

Change

I stand in the yard
Inhaling the deep dark scent of early November.
A heady, full-bodied fragrance
So different from the awakening, hopeful, earth-scents of
April.

Maple leaves, once green, then crimson,
Pile tattered and spotted onto my flower beds.
Leaves that swirled and floated in September
Now stick damply to the earth.

The short, life-giving summer has ended.
The long, cold winter lies in wait,
Ready to steal in under cover of moonlight.

Like the trees and earth,
I too prepare for change.
Not quite ready to bid farewell
To al fresco dinners and warm sunny days,
I resist
Then acquiesce.

Short days
Early darkness
Swirling flakes
Squeaky snow
Steaming bowls of soup
Popcorn by the fire
Mittens, hats, scarves, boots
Red noses and cheeks
Crisp sun sparkling on snowdrifts.

The earth,
Covered once more in a blanket of snow,
Slumbers
While I embrace seasons past, present and yet to come.

Nature's Jewelry

Yesterday I was sad.
Branches that just days ago
Dazzled me with leaves of red, yellow, gold
Stood naked
On a brilliantly colored carpet of lawn.

Overnight, Nature created one more show.
A sparkling display.
Last night's raindrops
Cling to every branch and twig.

This early November morning
Bedecked in shimmering, sparkling jewels,
Resplendent in the sun,
My trees stand proud.

And I,
I stand in awe
Once again.

Winter

Season Change

This morning
Fat, wet snowflakes glide gently onto our lawn
Autumn silently slips into winter.

No more warm mornings weeding flower beds
Bunnies no longer a worrisome threat to my hostas
Farmer's markets closed
Shorts and sandals packed away
Bug spray tossed
Salad suppers on the deck, ended
Lemonade gone

Time for comfy turtlenecks and wooly socks
Stew, chili and pot roast
Windows closed and locked against the coming snow
Air conditioner off
Furnace on
Hot chocolate
Cozy afghans

I'm remembering how much there is to love about winter.

Snow Day

Snow moved in across the city early this morning
Clouds heavy, forecast ominous.
By lunch time pine branches are laden with snow
Plows try to keep city streets open.

At 4:00 I start a fire in the fireplace
And sit by the big front window
Watching fat, swirling flakes
Drift into mounds on our yard.

Schools close early
I hear the slip and slide of cars
As drivers struggle through deep snow
To make their way home for dinner.

Beef stew simmers fragrantly on the stove
My house is cozy and warm.
I turn on lamps, and
Worry about those without warmth tonight.

We eat by the fireplace and watch the news.
Snow will end by mid evening,
Total accumulation for our area forecast at ten inches.
Heavy, wet, traffic-stopping, airplane-delaying snow.

At 10:00 I don boots, a warm jacket, wooly scarf and mittens
And step off my porch into snow that covers my boot tops.
Snow has stopped and the moon makes her entrance in the
sky.
Everything sparkles.
Silence.

Just me and my boots squeaking in fresh snow.
The cold bites my face and I burrow deeper into my scarf.
I trudge slowly down the middle of my street.
My boots leave the only marks in the new fallen snow.

Tomorrow I will shovel.
Tomorrow I will drive ever so cautiously on city streets
Tomorrow this won't appear to be quite so beautiful.

For now I will just breathe in. Look up. Breathe out.
Pause with wonder.
My world is a pristine, beautiful snow globe
In which I am privileged to live.

December

No month owns tradition like December does.
With a flip of my wall calendar from November to December
A wondrous season begins.

Gone are the orange, gold and brown candles.
Gone are the wooden pilgrims from the mantle.
Gone are the bouquets of bittersweet.
Gone is the centerpiece of gourds and mini pumpkins.
Gone, the dish of corn candy.

Boxes are pulled from storage,
Red and white candles for the mantle,
Bouquets of pine branches for the hearth,
Shiny silver balls and holly for the table,
Pine boughs to drape the stairs.

Familiar fragrances and tastes fill the house
Cranberry, pine, peppermint, bayberry
Sugar cookies, almond cookies, candy canes
Swedish sausage and herring.

Advent candles are lit and nativity sets tell of the wonder.
Music boxes and sound systems play well-loved melodies.
Gift lists are built, wrapping paper bought,
Shopping is done, packages wrapped and mailed.

Holiday greetings arrive
Updates and photos from friends near and far.
We buy our tree from the lot by the bank and
Hang a wreath on the front door.

We decorate tree, tables, shelves and sills
With cherished decorations
Precious keepsakes reminding of people and places.

Favorite books are stacked in a basket by the fireplace
Stockings are hung with care
Friends are invited in for hot beverages and cozy conversation

Our hearts grow a bit more generous
We work to find time to sit in stillness and wonder
We are once again enfolded in hope.

December.
Wondrous December.

December 27

How quiet our home is this late December morning.
No children laughing
No Lego building
No paper airplanes launching from the loft railing
No cookie crumbs on the stairs
No accumulating wine glasses by the sink
No Monopoly game on the table
No giggles in the sunroom
No bedheads and jammies

They all left yesterday.
Children gone.
Grandchildren gone.

Wonderful holiday memories of family remain.

Anticipation

They say it is on the way
Their faces serious and apprehensive
Plan ahead
Be careful out there
Just 22 hours until it hits.

I settle back into my chair and smile.
Just 22 hours until it hits?
I'm ready now!
Bring it on.

They say howling winds
Snow accumulating an inch an hour
Highways will be dangerous
It's not been this bad since the winter of '86
I'm ready.

Tomorrow my kitchen will smell of baking bread
And zesty vegetable soup
Three books are stacked next to my chair
A cozy afghan hangs on the arm
Wood is stacked on the hearth.

January blizzard.
Bring it on!

January Light

Sunlight bounces off acres of snow
A lone tree stands
A fat, black crayon-slash on stark, white paper.

Grandmothers
&
Grandmothering

AKA

Since you saw me last
I changed my name.
I have re-mastered the art of diapering, and
I play airplane games with spoons full of baby food.
I gave up my corner office
To become a cozy lap.
I build soaring castles out of blocks,
Sing soft lullabies and
Read Dr. Seuss.
Since you saw me last
I changed my name.

I'm now fondly known as Nana.

My Grandmas

Grandma K
Small town, small white house with a porch
Corn on the cob
Fresh tomatoes
Gladiolas of every color in her garden
Etched glass candy dish, always full
Crocheting lessons
Crisply ironed table runners
Coloring books and crayons
A fat, prickly cactus under her treadle sewing machine
African violets on every flat surface
Fresh-from-the-oven sweet rolls
Safe and comforting.

Grandma A
Small white house in the big city
Cinnamon bread from Donaldson's Tea Room
Swedish coffee pot, never empty
Chiming clock on the wall
Aroma of spices from her metal cupboard
Chicken and dumpling soup
Nubby green sofa
City bus to downtown
Television weather reports
Wooden covered photo albums
Hugs and laughter.

Nasturtiums and Fly Paper

Grandma's farm kitchen opened onto a small,
Screened-in back porch.
Grandpa left his muddy barn shoes here, and
Soaped his hands with strong Fels Naptha soap
Before coming into her kitchen.

Orange fly-paper strips
Unfurled from the old porch ceiling
Swayed in the summer breeze
Covered with stuck, captive flies.
The smelly strips held them prisoner.

A handmade pump-can of potent bug spray
Lay at rest on the screen sill,
A deterrent to any flying insect
With an eye toward reaching Grandma's kitchen counter.

The screens were covered
With red, orange and yellow climbing nasturtiums.
Their sweet fragrance mixed with
Odors of fly paper, Fels Naptha, and bug spray.
A peculiar smell.

It's been decades since I ran out of Grandma's back porch,
The wobbly screen door slamming as I ran to meet Grandpa.
But with a whiff of my garden nasturtiums today
I am immediately on that long ago porch,
Flying out the door and into Grandpa's arms.

Naming

"What was your name before it was Nana?" he asks.
"My real name is Kathy," I say.
The quick response sticks and niggles in my head.
My Name?

On the day of my birth
I am Kathleen Jo
Kathleen, for my maternal grandmother
Jo, for my paternal grandfather
Shortened in days to Kathy Jo.

There are love names in my family
I was "Spank" to my father
"Katy Kitten" to Aunt Wilma
"Kat" to Aunt Millie
"Dear One" to Grandma Katie.

In Junior High
I dropped the Jo
To become Kathy
Or Kathi
Or Kathie.

In High School
I reclaimed 'Jo' to become either
Kathy Jo, or Jo.
In college, KJ.

My husband calls me Kath
My brother makes up delicious ridiculous names
Every time he calls.

My favorite name was born in my late 20s
Kathy Jo took a backseat to Mommy
Then Mom, Momma, Momzer
And eventually, Nana.

Given name
Childhood names
Love names
Identity

Daughter
Granddaughter
Wife
Mother
Grandmother
Sister
Friend
Colleague
Neighbor
Mentor

Kathleen
Kathy Jo
Jo
KJ
Kath
Mom
Nana

Me.

Interesting Walks

"I've got our bag, Nana.
Are you ready to go?"

Out the door we go on another adventure.
We call them our "Interesting Walks."
We don't venture far into the neighborhood
Just a few streets away from home.

We pause at the first corner and debate whether
To go this way, or that way.
We choose left, take about fifteen steps
And then stop.

"So. What do we think is interesting here?"
"Well, there is a very, very big rock, Nana."
"How do you think it got here?
What could we play on this rock?
Is it cold or warm?"
Questions must be asked, some of them unanswerable.
"Take a picture of it, Nana so we will remember it."

Off we go another half block and stop again.
"What is interesting here?"
"There is green stuff growing on this tree!
There is a frog on the tree!
Somebody cut the tree with a knife!"
After we ask many questions
We take a pinch of tree moss and pop it into our bag.

Off we go again, this time making it a full block
Before he spies a pretty yellow flower
Growing out of the street drain.
"How in the world can it grow there?" I ask.

"Let's not pick it for our bag, it's too pretty."
And then a sprinkler system with a leak
Sending a spout of water high in the air,
Then eight stones stacked upon one another on the sidewalk.

We venture six blocks in all
Asking many questions about these interesting discoveries.
Our bag is filled with sticks, stones, a bead, a pine cone and
moss.

As we return home
My grandson says, "We probably won't tell everyone about
this.
They won't understand how interesting it was.
Can we go again tomorrow? Maybe a new way?"
I suggest that maybe we could go one night when it is dark.
"We could take a flashlight! I bet that would be interesting."

I bet it will be.

Meron's Table

She is three.
I've been invited to her table.
Before we can sit
We must first do a little preparation.
We don hot-pink boa scarves, and
I get a pink plastic tiara.
She chooses the purple gem-encrusted crown.
Bangle bracelets adorn our wrists.

She announces,
"Our table is ready, Ma'am."
The small white plastic table
Is covered with her mother's bright scarf.
There are two tea cups, two saucers,
A teapot of lemonade and
A small pink bowl of pretzel knots and Goldfish.

"Please, come sit!
How have you been?"
"I'm good. How are your babies?"
"Well, I have 15 you know!
And I know all their names."
"You must be very busy."
"I am. Hundreds of bottles and diapers and lots of crying."

"May I pour your tea?"
"Yes, of course! But it is very hot, so be careful.
I will eat the Goldfish and you may have the pretzels."
"Thank you. You are so generous."
"I am!"

"And its time now for you to leave.
Your granddaughter is waiting for you in the living room.
She would like to play Candy Land.
I'll see you again sometime soon."

"Thank you!
And I love you, you know."

"I know, Nana."

The Gift

Under the tree, gifts are arranged.
Big ones toward the back, little ones up front.
Beautifully wrapped boxes and bags
With glittery gift tags and swaths of red and green ribbon.

"Who is delivering the gifts?" I ask.
The six-year old eagerly
And with great importance claims the task.
"I'll be the deliverer, I know how to read the tags!"
"The job is yours."

One gift to Mom
One gift to Dad
One to a brother
One to Papa.

Tags are read,
Gifts are shaken, sniffed and squished.
Guesses are made about the contents,
Hopes arise.

Then the deliverer brings me mine.
"You need to open this one first, Nana.
It's from me and I wrapped it myself."

I had an inkling about that.
At least ten feet of tape was used in the endeavor
And a bold red marker boasts, "To Nana From Me"
I gently begin pulling tape off.

"I'll help!"
And the rapid tearing of wrapping paper begins.
"Should I tell you what it is?
"It's Art! And I made it for you. For your hall!"

Indeed it is art
Art of the most exquisite kind.
The kind you love the moment you lay eyes on it
Even if you cannot fathom what it is.

"Tell me about it! Did you make this?
I love it!"
"I just knew you would. Should we go hang it up now?"
"A splendid idea."

And as we walk hand in hand to the hallway
I know I have just received the best gift of the season.
There will be other gifts, carefully chosen, beautifully wrapped
Other gifts I will enjoy.

But this one is best.
The love of a grandchild
Wrapped up in messy tissue, tape and joy!

Baker Woman

Yeast, eggs, flour, salt, baking soda and milk
Lined up like soldiers on the counter.
Her big blue pottery mixing bowl and wooden spoon
Wait in readiness.

If it is Friday, it is bread-making day.
Long ago she made bread every day.
She does it now without looking at a recipe
Doesn't even take the recipe from the box.

Short and stout
Covered neck to knee
In her faded, flower-print, cover-all apron
The kind that goes over her head, ties in back,
Two giant pockets in front for
Hot pads and handkerchiefs.
This is the same outfit she wears most days
Whether baking, dusting, washing clothes or shaking rugs.

She begins.
Yeast in warm water
Eggs
A teaspoon of this, a tablespoon of that
Flour
She mixes and kneads the sticky dough
Plops it into a new bowl and covers it with a damp dishtowel.
It will sit on the counter in the sunshine until it rises,
Doubling in size.

It is now I make my move.
She is on the porch.
I stealthily sneak in, lift the dishtowel
And nab a nice chunk of warm dough.
Quick. Into my mouth.
I savor the texture and taste.
Only one chunk, or she will know.

Two hours later she shapes the dough
Into chubby balls and places them on a baking sheet
Brushes with butter and pops them into the oven.
Soon the whole house smells of baking bread.

She offers me a hot bun, fresh from the oven.
Heavenly.
She asks which I like better,
The dough or the baked bun.
Caught!

Later in life I will ask her for the recipe.
I, too, want to be a baker woman.
Her hands shake too badly to write the recipe for me
So she tells me over the phone.
I'm doomed.
"Add enough flour until it feels right.
Two eggs or three depending on the size.
Mix ingredients until dough is not quite sticky."

I will try, Grandma,
But some things may be better left as delicious memories.

When Did This Happen?

I sit on the deck overhearing a conversation.
A small child is negotiating with his parent
To achieve a later bed time, just for tonight.

"Do you think this is a good idea?"
"Yes."
"Can you tell me why you need to stay up later?
Will you still be ready to get out of bed in the morning if you
stay up late?"
The conversation goes on.

It seems like only yesterday
That I had the same conversation with my own child.
Now my child is the parent.

Absolute joy to watch one's children parent.
Creating boundaries when it isn't fun,
Praising for small things done well,
Crazy happy for bigger things done well,
Saying 'No' when it must be said,
Hugging generously,
Helping the child make good decisions,
Being responsible.

I'm so proud.
But it was just yesterday when I was the young parent
So how is it possible I am the grandparent?

What Do You See?

I walk with the grandchildren
They see so much more than I.

I see the busy street
Hear the helicopter above
Feel the mugginess of August
Hear a siren in the distance.

They see a ladybug on a leaf and stop to chat
Pick an earthworm from the sidewalk and put it in the grass
Find treasure in a small coral-colored stone
A butterfly lands on a small outstretched hand.

Can I learn to see again?

Kitchens

Grandma's kitchen was simple.
No pictures on the walls except
The Farm Bureau calendar.
The countertop was linoleum, worn and non-descript.
In front of the sink a woven rag rug.
A mason jar with flowers sat on the window sill.
Her stove was old, and held
Pottery pig salt and pepper shakers and
A pottery cat pitcher.

Grandma cooked and baked with
Salt and pepper,
Allspice, nutmeg and cinnamon.
She fried meats and vegetables in butter or shortening,
Her bread was unparalleled.

Her menus included:
> Crunchy deep-fried chicken, mashed potatoes and
> gravy
> Tender roast beef, mashed potatoes and gravy
> Tasty pork roast, mashed potatoes and gravy
> Homemade dinner rolls
> Canned beans, pickles, peaches, and pears
> Pies

My kitchen is lovely.
Art hangs on the walls along with
A calendar I bought in Tuscany.
Grandma's pottery cat sits on a shelf.
My granite countertop shines, and
A fat bouquet of fresh flowers sits on the island.

I cook with
Cumin, curry and cilantro,
Herbs de Provence and dill.
Lemon pepper, garlic,
Peanut sauce and Dijon.
I sauté in olive oil.

My menus include:
Greek salads
Curried chicken with rice
Shrimp and pasta in peanut sauce
Baked chicken with artichoke hearts
Pita chips and hummus
Fresh fruit
Chocolate fondue.

Kitchens.
Old fashioned or sparkly new
The place where family and friends gather
To laugh, share stories, give thanks and break bread.
Making delicious memories.

The Recipe Card

The card has been in my recipe box for over 40 years
Written in pencil on a 3x5 white index card
Blotched with grease and stained with vanilla.

I know the recipe by heart,
Wouldn't even need to take it out of the box.
But when I do, she is standing right beside me,
Her short, plump, grandmotherly self
Always most comfortable when baking.

I could frame it
But then it would be a piece of art
Instead of a deliciously warm memory of childhood.

Musings

Bookshelves and Leather Chairs

Majestic oaks wrap their arms around
The tall, stately, columned structure
On a corner in my hometown.
Big, heavy, double doors open to a peaceful stillness
That smells of books, old wood and leather chairs.
My childhood public library.

At five, I chose books from the Children's Room.
Small round tables, small chairs and short bookshelves
Just my size.

At twelve, I moved up to a new world,
Shelves stacked floor to ceiling with fiction, biography,
Travel, non-fiction.

At fifteen, my debate partner and I
Did impressive research on Saturdays
While watching the boys at the next table.

At seventeen, I left for the sprawling libraries
Of universities and big cities.

At fifty I returned to reminisce.

The stately old building remains, but its
Shelves now hold old green Coke bottles,
45 rpm records,
Pottery like Grandma's,
One shelf of worn, tattered, old books.
Familiar smells, gone.

Not a library any longer, but
A dusty, small town antique shop.

Why am I so sad?
Why, of all the libraries I have loved,
Is this the one that holds my heart?

Magic Card

I carry a magic card in my wallet.
Its powers take me anywhere in the world.
It sanctions time-travel.

With it I have visited
Vineyards in Provence,
Antebellum homes in Natchez,
The icy beauty of Hudson Bay,
A cabin in the pines,
Spring in Paris,
And a hippopotamus-filled river in Africa.

I have marched with suffragists,
Sailed across the Atlantic to a new world,
Witnessed wars and discrimination,
Grown pineapples in Hawaii,
Explored the Nile,
Dined with the Queen.

The card causes me to shiver with fear,
Or laugh, while tears streak my face.
With a gleam in my eye, and an 'Aha!' I solve the mystery.
In grief, I ache with sadness.
My heart fills with emotion too deep for words.

This card works wherever I have an address.
Magic. Sheer Magic.
My library card.

City Views

Sleek glass and metal office buildings brush the city sky.
Waiting for a green light, I admire their aloof elegance.
Well-dressed professionals spin through revolving doors
On their way to important decisions.

My gaze follows the architectural lines up and up.
Moments before the stoplight changes,
My eyes come back to earth
And rest on an old red-brick, two-story apartment building
Defiantly holding its place between two towering skyscrapers.

A second floor window is open and
A white curtain flutters in the breeze.
An elderly woman in her faded bathrobe
Sits in the window with her cat
Our eyes meet
I smile and nod. She nods.
Who is she?

I'd love to hear her story.

Invisible Me

The meeting has ended.
Exhausted from days of decision-making,
Strategizing, negotiating,
I'm on the shuttle to the airport.

Two men in front of me
Discuss financial planning strategies,
A young woman frantically sends texts,
Two nuns in habits talk quietly,
An elderly man appears to be very nervous.
None of them expect me to interact.

The shuttle driver calls out my airline.
I step out into the brisk, late November day,
Get my bag, tip the driver, smile.
I step through the doors toward the check-in counter.

The baggage check kiosk wants only
My airline card and boarding pass.
The TSA-approved security line
Moves swiftly and mechanically.
Briefcase on the conveyor belt,
I step through the metal detector.
I'm in!

I'm in 'airport disappearance' mode.
No one sees me,
I am alone in a mass of moving humanity.
My airport self sighs audibly,
I am now invisible.
No one cares what I think,
No one expects a decision from me.

No one tries to sway my thinking,
No one needs me to be or to do,
No eye contact,
Few smiles.
Invisible.

I sigh.
Buy a box of popcorn
Settle into a slightly worn,
Uncomfortable chair at an empty gate.
I stare into space.
Too exhausted to read,
I hold my novel but don't even crack the cover.
I watch jumbo jets glide down the taxiway
While carts and trucks ready planes on the tarmac.

I am invisible.
Wrapped in a cocoon of
White noise,
Jet engines,
Public address announcements.

Invisible.
My normal extrovert self
Delights in this retreat into solitude.
I sigh deeply. Again.
Invisible.

The Harbor

I stand looking out over the harbor,
Spring sunshine warm on my back.
Colorful sailboats bob on waves near shore,
Hulking ships fly flags unknown to me, and
Rest secure at giant piers.
Tourist shops and marine supply stores conduct brisk business.

Who will sail today, I wonder.
What ships will leave this port for days at sea?
No lines. No booths selling tickets to holiday destinations.
No crowds waving goodbye and bon voyage.
Just me. On the massive pier, gazing out to the horizon.

Why then, tears?
I see what isn't here, but was.

My family left this Swedish harbor 116 years ago today
Bound for the land of promise.
Otto and Gustava, children
Carl Gustav, Anna, Elin and baby Vilhelm.
Whom did they leave?
Who stood on this pier, arms outstretched in farewell
Grieving as the ship steamed from shore?

Did she want to go?
Take her children from all they knew?
Whom did she leave? A mother? A sister? A best friend?
Did she ache with loss, and tremble with fear of the unknown?
Did she comfort her children, her tears mingling with theirs
As the Homeland disappeared?

Or was she craving adventure,
Eager for a better life, a new start?
Were her treasured books tucked in among pieces
Of precious china?
Did she stand on the deck, confident and impatient,
Heart racing with excitement?
Did the children catch her mood
And dance in circles around her long skirts?
Did she smile at him, sharing hope and promises?

The harbor wraps me in wonder.
I feel my roots.
Tears.

(Gothenburg Sweden, March 27, 2007)

Heartbeat

Long forgotten and set aside
It sat on a dusty shelf in their attic.
The attic fascinated me,
Filled with keepsakes of my new husband's family.

The mantle clock was plain dark wood with brass trim.
I asked about its history.
My husband shrugged his shoulders,
My new mother-in-law smiled,
And said, "It was a 25th wedding anniversary gift."
Touching it, I smiled and said it was lovely.

A day later the clock sat on her dining room table.
Did I want it?
Could I? Could we?

A few months later it came to our home
And was lovingly placed on our living room mantle.
I wound it tightly and tapped the pendulum to start the ticking.

Decades later, and countless different shelves and addresses
I continue to wind it tightly and tap its pendulum.
It is the heartbeat of our home.
I hear the rhythmic *tick, tick, tick* on a quiet afternoon.
I hear it chime three times, four times, on a sleepless night.
I am reminded to move a little faster at the 'half past' chime.

I smile,
Wind it tightly once again.
This old, old clock
Keeping the heartbeat of a family through generations.

Mapping

A faded, tattered, dusty, world map
Is tacked crookedly to the wall of my rented beach house.

I pause before it and it pulls me in.
It seduces me with
Cities, rivers, countries and seas
I've never encountered.
Marrakech
Dakar
Cusco
Isle of Man

If I visited there,
What foods would I enjoy?
Where would I go?
Would the music sing in my soul?
Would people in the market smile at me?
What local handcrafts would I find?
What smells would forever remind me of that place?

The map causes me to dream.
It causes me to plan.
Oh yes, there are tantalizing adventures ahead!

Missing Word

I'm looking for a word today.
One word giving clarity to my thoughts.
The thesaurus lends no clues.
My alphabet games draw a blank.

One word.
I'm looking for just one word.
It eludes my grasp.
Writer's block?
Or just being sixty-something?

Yes, Please

Six years-
Peanut butter and honey sandwiches
Chocolate cake with fluffy white frosting

Nine Years-
Grandma A's cinnamon bread, Grandma K's banana bread

Twelve years-
Pizza, thick chocolate malts, crispy fries

Sixteen years —
Burgers and fries, pizza

Twenty One years-
Beef fondue, lasagna, pizza

Thirty Five years-
Steaks on the grill, pizza, wine

Fifty Five years-
Crab legs, twice baked potatoes, pizza

Sixty Five years-
Seafood salad, crunchy bread, thin crust pizza, wine,
Grilled fish, burgers, Maid Rites, chocolate anything,
Chocolate chip cookie dough, Diet Coke, chardonnay,
Peanut butter and banana sandwiches, deviled eggs,
Chips and dip, cheese enchiladas, guacamole, BLTs

I'll have another, please.

Midnight

Sleep eludes me.
So sleepy at 3:00 this afternoon
I could have napped for an hour.
I didn't.

Now in my bed
I look out the window
And watch as moonlight dances between tree branches.
I hear a cricket. Or two. Or three.
Soft summer sounds.

A train whistles in the darkness.
Where is it going?
Did I close the patio door?
Should I bake cookies to take to my friend?
Where is that yellow plate I use for cookies?
I haven't used it all summer.
I like it.

Kids are growing so fast.
We haven't taken a family photo this year.
We can take one in the fall leaves.
I should make a list of things to do before fall comes.
We have plenty of firewood for more wiener roasts.
S'mores would be good.

I need to buy birthday cards.
Lots of birthdays in the next two months.
Do I have cards stashed in my desk?
I will check.

I'm thirsty.
If I get up to get a drink
I will really be awake.
Sleep eludes me.

It's 12:20.

Preference

He walks down the sidewalk,
A stunning bouquet of long-stemmed pink roses
Carried tenderly in his arms.
Will they achieve his hopes?
Will she exclaim, tear up and throw her arms around him?
I hope so.

And me?
I'd rather have a tousled bunch of wild flowers.
A bouquet of simple sunflowers in brilliant yellow,
Or a chubby vase filled with deep pink peonies.
I would.

The Box

The small cardboard box was worn and shabby
With a cover that didn't close.
Corners rounded, no longer square,
The contents broken and ugly.
It sat forgotten, dusty,
Unused and worthless on the shelf.
No miracles left inside.

The child bumped it while reaching
For her flowered teapot.
She pulled out the box and scattered
Its contents across the wooden floor.
Grimacing, she sighed.

In her small hand the broken, tattered crayons
Were a perfect fit.
She picked up only three:
Sky Blue, Raspberry Red and Sea Foam Green.
Flowers. Umbrellas. Kites.

And one Raspberry Red elephant.
She created. She smiled.

Ha!
The miracle was just waiting to be discovered!

Letter to Myself at 14

Dear Kathy,
You want so much to be in the 'in' group
Ninth grade is hard
You're all elbows and awkwardness
Your pointy, harlequin glasses make you look like an owl
That perm doesn't work when you shower after gym class
Be patient.

Gracefulness will float in on you any month now.
Your shyness is ready to bubble into leadership
You'll find your voice and your place
You'll be comfortable with who you are.
Be patient.

Some dark, deep and difficult life-days lie ahead.
You will survive.
You'll even thrive.
But it will take time.
I know, 9th graders want instant results.
Deep breath. Deep breath.
Stop and smell the peonies.

The 'in' girls.
Well, they won't be 'in' forever.
And the cute guy?
He does know who you are.
Do you?

 Love,
        Kathy

Renovations

A visit to the city.
I check in to a hotel I have stayed in countless times
Today, renovations have transformed it with
A shiny, sleek, new lobby
A bar with tall tables and elegant lighting
Luxurious guest rooms
New linens, drapes, furniture.

Gone are the familiar cozy arm chairs.
In their place, stylish, uncomfortable imposters
Beautiful but different.

I have come to this hotel for twenty years.
How many times has change transformed me?
Did I start shiny, sleek and stylish,
And am now comfortable and cozy?
Transformed and yet familiar?
Renovated?

Book Lover

I'm home from the book shop
My bag stuffed full
New treasures abound.

Books for the grandchildren
A mystery for my husband
Three birthday cards
And two books just for me.

I began looking for my choices
On the long shelves of new releases
Looking for some of the latest, best reviewed books,
Front covers caught my eye
I read synopses on back covers and inside flaps,
I pondered, I debated.
None here suited my fancy.

My first choice I discovered in the Travel Section,
One of my favorite aisles.
A travel journal written by an American woman
Traveling in Italy in the late 40s.
Oh, I must have this!

The second, I found in the Fiction Section
An early work by a well-loved author,
It promises to take me deep into a delicious,
Complicated family.
I must have this, too.

Now home, I empty my canvas tote.
Brand new, neither book appears to have been opened.
The bindings crack when I open the front covers,
Reminding me of the first day of school
When the teacher taught us the proper way
To open a new textbook.
I learned well.

After properly opening,
I lift the book to my nose and inhale 'book fragrance'
Paper, ink, glue.
One of the most delicious fragrances ever created.
I run my hand over an open page,
Loving the feel of the paper's weight and fiber.
Do I have time to settle into my favorite chair right now?
Can I postpone my 'to do' list until tomorrow?
Not a difficult choice at all.
I settle in and the writer begins her magic
Skillfully transporting me in time and place.

Being a book lover
Is not complicated at all.
It involves my eyes, my nose, my hands, my mind,
A delightful dose of expectation for the hours ahead
And a sigh of joy in how I choose to spend today.
And who knows,
Maybe tomorrow too!

Dancing in the Sanctuary Glass

He is about a year old.
I watch him in his mother's arms
From across the crowded sanctuary.
His attention is held for a moment by a lit candle,
Then by flowers on the altar.
He wiggles.
He pats his mother's face.
He munches a few Cheerios from a blue plastic container.
His sisters ignore him.
He squeals at the end of the hymn.
His mother shooshes him and gently bounces him in her lap.

He fusses a bit.
She moves out of the pew and
Walks him toward the back corner,
The corner where bright sunlight shines through stained glass.
His tousled blond hair
Catches a rainbow of purple, gold and red.
He sees the color on his hand first.
Looking up at his mother as if to say,
"Where did this come from?"
He turns his hand over and over.
The rainbow stays.

She sits on the bench under the window
And helps him stand to explore.
He stands tentatively and reaches out with one finger.
He touches the stained glass,
Pulls his hand back as if burned.

Tries again.
Then sees the rainbow on his arm, his shoe, his belly.
He giggles.
He dances in awe.

His mother's eyes light up as she watches his discovery unfold.
Dancing in the sanctuary glass
Dancing in the light of God.

The Vanity

The aged, scarred vanity sits in the corner of the bedroom
Its oversized, round mirror smudged black with time.
I sit on its small, upholstered bench
Combing my hair and checking my makeup before I go.

I wonder who else sat here looking in this mirror.
What were her stories?
Did she sit here with anticipation?
Tears? Dreams?

Who spilled the cherry red nail polish
In the top right-hand drawer?
What was she rushing to?
Who scratched 'DK loves J' in the middle left drawer?
Was it an impulse accomplished with great hope,
Or with a sigh?

A key is taped to the back of the bottom right drawer.
Tape, brown and fraying but still holding the small gold key.
Jewelry box key? Diary key?
Why didn't she take it when the vanity moved on?
When she moved on?

What clues will I unknowingly leave?
Who will be next to read this vanity?

George

Tomorrow, George the Window Cleaner comes.
With tall spindly ladders he climbs further than I would dare
Cleaning screens and glass
Washing a season out the door.

With buckets, sponges and squeegees
He destroys months of accumulated dirt
From storms and wind.
A season of spider web homes disappear.
Within minutes windows sparkle and
Brilliant sunlight fills our rooms.

George is part of our 'season change' ritual.
As surely as the clocks will be set ahead or back
In spring and fall,
As surely as flower beds are prepared for growth or rest,
As surely as our menu moves from pot roast to grilling,
He arrives to call a new season through our windows and into
our home.

Necessities

My purse carries just a few things:
Smart phone in hot pink case
Colored pens
Leather-bound paper calendar
Cinnamon gum
Credit cards
Library card
Insurance card
Driver's license
Bookstore card
Family photos
Lipstick – two tubes
Cash – for parking or a Diet Coke
Coffee shop card – a latte
Sunglasses
Keys – house and car
Emory board
Tylenol, Aspirin, Aleve
Seven cough drops
Tissues
Comb
One Tootsie Roll

Just in case.

Thank You Notes

My desktop -
Neatly organized and clean
Framed photos, a small pink antique vase for pens

My note cards -
Intentionally small
Intended for few words

Stamp choices -
Summer flowers?
A landscape?

My ancient address book -
Messy with cross outs
Cramped additions

The gift list for my thank you notes -
Some gifts are appreciated
Some not so much

Procrastination.
Maybe tomorrow.

My Bench

Our arboretum is beautiful.
Trees, flowers, herbs, walking paths, waterfalls and ponds.
Spring, summer and fall I visit often.
Driving through the gates all my senses kick in.
I could wander for hours and enjoy every blooming thing,
But I have a favorite place.

I drive the winding road to a gravel parking lot.
Grabbing my tote, I walk with purpose up the incline
Away from the road
Away from the car park
Away to the "Tall Grasses"
To my special bench.

The huge meadow holds countless varieties of grasses.
In early June they are knee high,
By August, many are higher than I can reach.
On three sides, my meadow has walls of pines.
The fourth side is open
To a wide rolling meadow and endless sky.

My faded old wooden bench faces the wide open sky.
It could use a good sanding
And a coat of varnish.
It isn't pretty,
But when I see it, I smile.
It is mine.
It chose me almost ten years ago.
As I happened into the Tall Grasses,
It called to me.

This bench is my writing place
My pondering place
My praying place
My do nothing place.

An ant paces back and forth on the arm of my bench.
A fat bumble bee lands heavily on the shrub behind me.
Is he looking over my shoulder to offer suggestions?
I hear a cricket or two or ten.
Birds sing melodies just for me.

I'm often here alone.
Few take time from the showy flowers
To wander through Tall Grasses.

Shhhhh.
I'm sitting on my bench.

Always a Lake Girl

Down the gravel road,
Take a right at the blue house.
Left at the fork and there it is,
The summer cabin.
Our rental for two weeks.

We pull suitcases up the wooden steps
And unlock the door.
My eyes take it all in.
Yes, this will do quite nicely.

I unpack necessities,
Then grab sunscreen, bug spray, a bottle of water.
The dock beckons.
Like a child, I run with abandon to the water's edge.

Deep breathe.
My lungs welcome the lake air,
My feet escape their shoes,
Worries begin to drift away.

The smell of earth and water, familiar since childhood.
I know this lake land,
It is in my bones,
It is in my heart.

No grand expectations of water sports,
I just need a beach,
A dock.

My soul begins to fill.
I am most whole here.
My heart knows this.
This is where I belong.

About The Author

Kathy Kunkel Magnus grew up in the heart of the lakes region in Central Minnesota. A graduate of the University of Minnesota, she enjoyed a long professional career in the Lutheran church, serving in a variety of executive positions in regional, national and global work. Her writing has been published in several magazines but this is her first book. She and her husband Richard, reside in the Minneapolis area and spend the cold, icy, Minnesota winters in Southern California where she has come to love the ocean in addition to being a 'Lake Girl.' They have two adult children and seven grandchildren. Life is good with family, friends, travel, volunteering, reading and writing.